My Memories and Legacy

Bright
COMMUNICATIONS

Printed in the United States of America

Published in Hellertown, PA

Cover and interior design by Jennifer Giandomenico

For more information or to place bulk orders, contact the publisher at Jennifer@BrightCommunications.net.

BrightCommunications.net

To you and your happy memories!

Contents

How to Use This Book

This book is designed to help you record and share your memories and legacy. You can fill this out by yourself or with a family member, friend, or caregiver.

First, this book explains benefits to preserving your memory and legacy. Then it offers tips on how to make time to do this and how to help someone who might be interviewing you.

Then this book includes 12 do-it-yourself memory and legacy preserving projects. You can fill these out right in this book, or you can write your answers on other paper or a notebook.

If you wish, you can hire the team at Bright Communications to interview you or to create beautifully designed keepsake editions of any of these projects.

Do you have a book idea? We also can help you write and publish your book, including children's books, young adult books, novels, memoirs, and nonfiction books.

For more information, contact Jennifer Bright, founding CEO of Bright Communications, at jennifer@brightcommunications.net or 610-216-0913.

The Benefits to Memory Preservation

The benefits to preserving your memories and sharing your story are huge:

To you:

- Helping you to remember your past
- Keeping your memories alive
- Remembering things better
- Having an outlet for your thoughts and feelings
- Getting memories "out of your head"
- Preserving memories for your family
- Keeping memory function
- Increasing cognition
- Helping to monitor and track cognition
- Discovering new ways to preserve and share your memories and story

To your family:

- Providing access to your memories
- Preserving your memories
- Saving time by having professional help accessing, recording, and preserving memories
- Helping to organize memorabilia
- Encouraging you to organize and pare down collections

To your caregivers:

- Providing opportunities for activities
- Helping seniors to "live in the past"—a happy, comfortable time for them
- Increasing and preserving seniors' cognition
- Generating income for a senior facility

Tips for Making Time

- Choose the best time of day for you.
- Find the best place to write.
- Schedule it in your calendar.
- Set a reminder for yourself.
- Invite a friend to remind you about it or to check in with you.
- Ask someone to work with you.
- Plan to work for a short time each session, but continue if you are enjoying it!

Tips for Being Interviewed

- Remember, your stories are important! Sharing them will help preserve your history and allows you to pass your wisdom along to others.
- Choose the best time of day for you to talk. Some folks are morning people, and others are more comfortable talking later in the day.
- Make sure you're comfortable as you're chatting. Choose a favorite chair, have a soothing beverage to sip, and relax.
- Ask the interviewer to record your conversation so you can be sure they're getting the facts right. Consider suggesting that they also take notes as a back-up.
- If you're uncomfortable talking about certain aspects of your life or find that some topics are too difficult for you to discuss, you can stop. It's up to you what you tell the interviewer.
- Be prepared if the conversation becomes emotional. Let the interviewer know if you need more time to talk about sensitive subjects. It's okay to ask them to come back to a touchy topic at another time or avoid certain topics altogether.
- If you're getting tired, let the interviewer know. You might want to limit your interviews to 15 to 30 minutes. It's okay if it takes a few sessions to tell your stories.

My Favorite Things

Favorite color: _____

Favorite holiday: _____

Favorite animal: _____

Favorite song: _____

Favorite book: _____

Favorite car: _____

Favorite movie: _____

Favorite food: _____

Favorite sport: _____

Favorite sports team: _____

Favorite TV show: _____

Favorite season: _____

Favorite smell: _____

Favorite hobby: _____

Favorite time of day: _____

Favorite candy:_____

Favorite flower or plant: _____

 # Letter to My Loved One

Dear _____

_____

_____

_____

_____

_____

_____

_____

_____

_____

_____

_____

_____

_____

_____

_____

_____

_____

_____

_____

_____

_____

Love, _____

My Family Tree

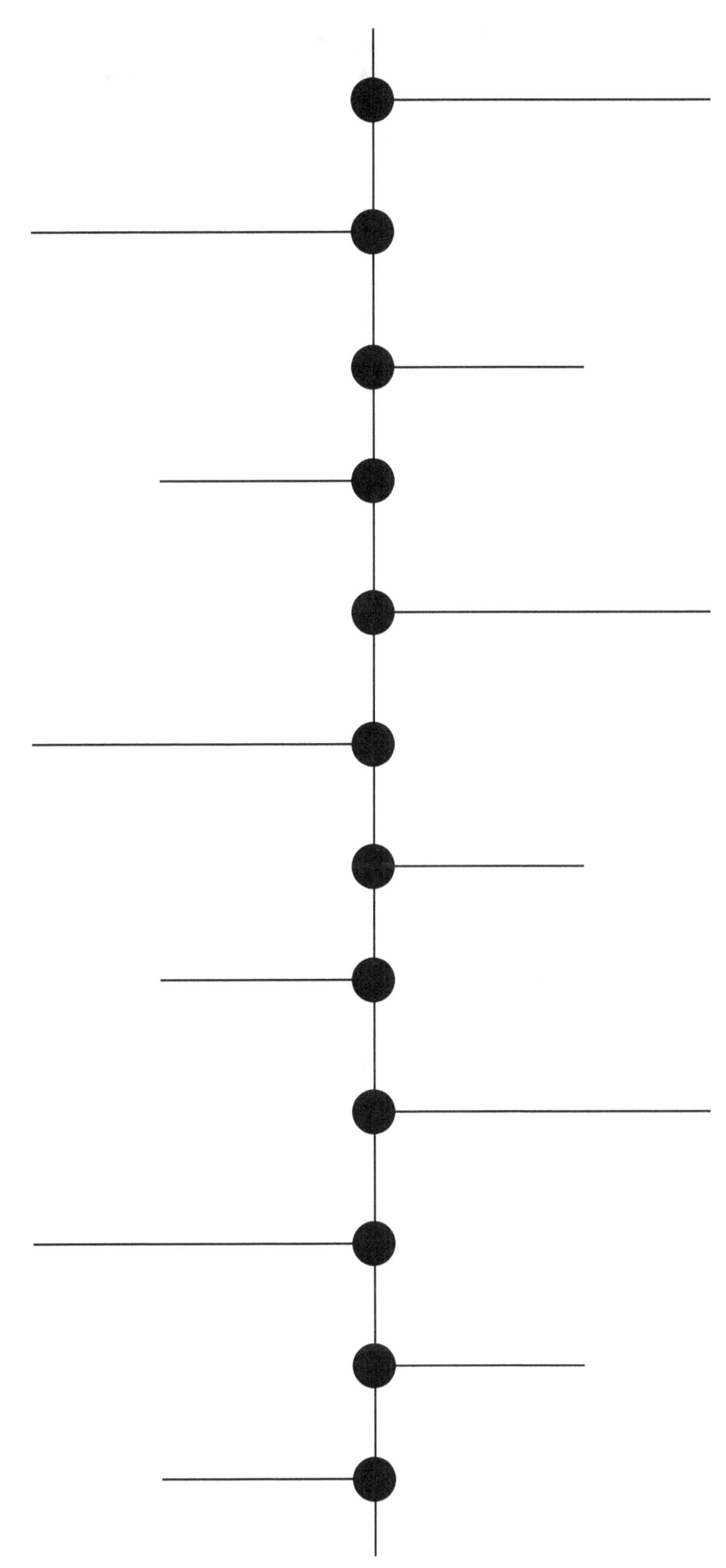

 # Milestone Letter

Please give this letter to my loved one upon: _____

Dear _____

_____

_____

_____

_____

_____

_____

_____

_____

_____

_____

_____

_____

_____

_____

_____

_____

_____

_____

_____

_____

Love, _____

Favorite Recipe

Recipe: _____

Ingredients:

_____ _____
_____ _____
_____ _____
_____ _____
_____ _____
_____ _____
_____ _____
_____ _____
_____ _____
_____ _____

Directions: _____

_____
_____
_____
_____
_____
_____

Memories about this recipe: _____

_____

The Essence of My Loved Ones

Rather than recording a memory, here's a place to remember how your loved ones made you feel.

Name: _____

Relationship to me: _____

His or her essence: _____

_____

Name: _____

Relationship to me: _____

His or her essence: _____

_____

Name: _____

Relationship to me: _____

His or her essence: _____

_____

Name: _____

Relationship to me: _____

His or her essence: _____

_____

Name: _____

Relationship to me: _____

His or her essence: _____

_____

The Soundtrack of My Life

The first song I remember: _____

_____

My first favorite song: _____

Songs my loved ones sang to me:_____

_____

_____

My favorite holiday song: _____

Songs or hymns from my faith: _____

_____

_____

Songs I remember from my school days: _____

_____

_____

My prom theme or other song I remember dancing to: _____

My wedding song: _____

Songs that always inspire me:_____

_____

Songs I sang to children: _____

_____

_____

My favorite songs: _____

_____

_____

My Tips and Tricks

Here are some things I wanted to share. _____

_____

_____

_____

_____

If you're looking for these things, here's where to find them!

- _____   _____

- _____   _____

- _____   _____

- _____   _____

- _____   _____

- _____   _____

Each week, remember to: _____

_____

Each month, remember to: _____

_____

Each year, remember to: _____

_____

Other tips: _____

_____

_____

_____

Short Biography

What is your full name? _____

Have you ever gone by other names? _____

Have you had any nicknames? _____

What is your favorite:

Color: _____

Food: _____

Song: _____

TV show: _____

Movie: _____

Animal: _____

Holiday: _____

When and where were you born? _____

_____

What was your childhood family like (mother, father, brothers, sisters?) _____

_____

_____

What was your childhood home like? _____

_____

What's your earliest memory?_____

_____

As a child, what did you want to be when you grew up? _____

_____

What was a typical day like for you when you were in elementary school? _____

_____

What were middle school and high school like for you?_____

_____

How did you celebrate holidays when you were young? _____

_____

What was your favorite meal growing up? Do you have the recipe? _____

_____

What are some of your memories of your parents and grandparents? _____

_____

What did you do for fun as a kid/teenager/young adult/parent?_____

_____

What did you worry about as a kid/teenager/young adult/parent?_____

_____

How many states and/or countries have you lived in? _____

_____

What was your favorite place to live? _____

_____

How many states and/or countries have you visited? _____

What was your favorite place to visit? _____

What was a pivotal experience in your life that changed you for the better? How?

_____

_____

What did you worry about most as a parent that didn't actually materialize? _____

_____

What didn't you worry about enough? _____

_____

What was your favorite moment of parenting? _____

_____

What was your favorite recipe or thing to cook? _____

_____

What is your most cherished family tradition?_____

_____

Have you had any major health challenges or surgeries? What was that like? _____

_____

_____

How has technology influenced your life? _____

_____

What have you liked best about your life so far? _____

_____

What is your happiest or proudest moment? _____

_____

What advice did your grandparents or parents give you that you remember best?

_____

_____

If you had the power to solve one and only one problem in the world, what would it be and why? _____

_____

What do you see as historical milestones for America during your lifetime? Where were you when each took place?_____

_____

What stories do you remember your parents telling about their parents? _____

_____

What are your greatest accomplishments? _____

_____

What are your biggest passions? _____

_____

What was the happiest thing that ever happened to you (or a few examples?) _____

_____

_____

What was the event or circumstance that caused you to use your greatest strength?

_____

_____

Were there forks in your life path that you now wish you had taken the other choice?

_____

_____

What was the greatest gift you ever received (or a few examples?) _____

_____

What was your greatest risk that resulted in success? failure? _____

_____

What's on your bucket list? What have you scratched off your bucket list and what do you still want to do? _____

_____

What did you do for fun with your friends when you were young? _____

_____

What was your first job? _____

What did you like to spend your money on? _____

What was your faith like? _____

What else would you like to share? _____

_____

_____

_____

_____

_____

_____

 # Journal in a Jar

Cut along the dotted lines, and then answer the questions at your own pace. Put the completed slips into a jar or other container.

- -

What is your full name? _____

- -

Have you ever gone by other names? _____

- -

Have you had any nicknames? _____

- -

What is your favorite:

Color: _____

Food: _____

Song: _____

TV show: _____

Movie: _____

Animal: _____

Holiday: _____

- -

When and where were you born? _____

_____

- -

What was your childhood family like (mother, father, brothers, sisters?) _____

_____

- -

What was your childhood home like? _____

_____

What's your earliest memory?_____

_____

As a child, what did you want to be when you grew up? _____

_____

What was a typical day like for you when you were in elementary school? _____

_____

What were middle school and high school like for you?_____

_____

How did you celebrate holidays when you were young? _____

_____

What was your favorite meal growing up? Do you have the recipe? _____

_____

What are some of your memories of your parents and grandparents? _____

_____

What did you do for fun as a kid/teenager/young adult/parent?_____

_____

What did you worry about as a kid/teenager/young adult/parent? _____

_____

How many states and/or countries have you lived in? _____

_____

What was your favorite place to live? _____

_____

How many states and/or countries have you visited? _____

What was your favorite place to visit? _____

What was a pivotal experience in your life that changed you for the better? How?

_____

_____

What did you worry about most as a parent that didn't actually materialize? _____

_____

What didn't you worry about enough? _____

_____

What was your favorite moment of parenting? _____

_____

What was your favorite recipe or thing to cook? _____
_____

What is your most cherished family tradition? _____
_____

Have you had any major health challenges or surgeries? What was that like? _____
_____
_____

How has technology influenced your life? _____
_____

What have you liked best about your life so far? _____
_____

What is your happiest or proudest moment? _____
_____

What advice did your grandparents or parents give you that you remember best?
_____
_____

If you had the power to solve one and only one problem in the world, what would it be and why?
_____

What do you see as historical milestones for America during your lifetime? Where were you when each took place? _____

_____

What stories do you remember your parents telling about their parents? _____

_____

What are your greatest accomplishments? _____

_____

What are your biggest passions? _____

_____

What was the happiest thing that ever happened to you (or a few examples?) _____

_____

_____

What was the event or circumstance that caused you to use your greatest strength?

_____

_____

Were there forks in your life path that you now wish you had taken the other choice?

_____

_____

What was the greatest gift you ever received (or a few examples?) _____

_____

What was your greatest risk that resulted in success? failure? _____

_____

What's on your bucket list? What have you scratched off your bucket list and what do you still want to do? _____

_____

What did you do for fun with your friends when you were young? _____

_____

What was your first job? _____

What did you like to spend your money on? _____

What was your faith like? _____

What else would you like to share? _____

_____

_____

_____

_____

My Kiss Goodbye

About me: _____

_____

_____

_____

_____

My fondest memories: _____

_____

_____

_____

My most cherished wish: _____

_____

_____

_____

I'll always remember: _____

_____

_____

_____

Please remember me by: _____

_____

_____

_____

Create Keepsake Editions

If you wish, you can hire the team at Bright Communications to interview you or to create beautifully designed keepsake editions of any of these projects.

Short Bio:

A 60-minute interview with one of our writers, from which we will create a double-sided, 1000-word, beautifully designed keepsake story. $800

Journal in a Jar:

We can interview you, then transform the letter into a beautifully designed keepsake: $200

Letter to a Loved One:

We'll help you write your letter, then create a beautifully designed keepsake to gift: $100

Milestone Letters:

We can interview you to write the letters, then create a set of beautifully designed milestone letters to gift: $200 per letter

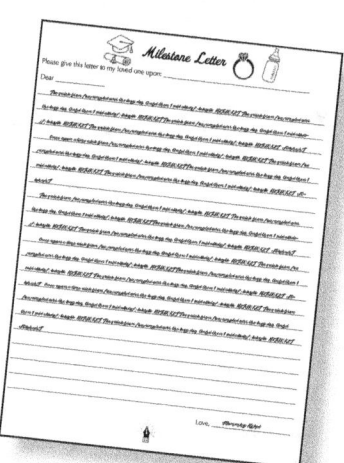

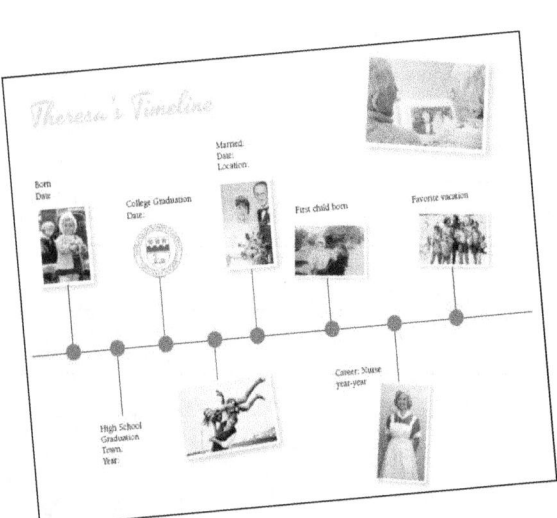

Life Timeline:

We can interview you and create timeline of their lives. $300

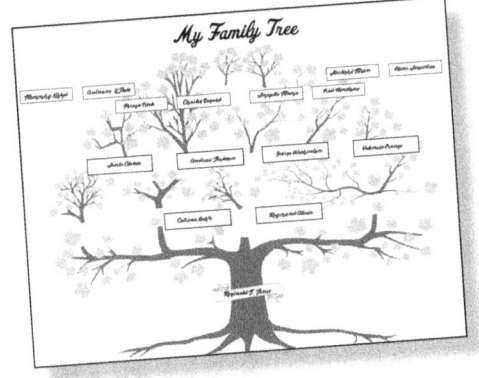

Family Tree:

We can interview you and create a
family tree going back several generations. $300

Recipe Collections:

We can help you to organize and gather their
favorite recipes in 10 one-page recipe "cards." $1,000

Your Favorite Things:

We can work with you to describe and remember some
of your favorite things and design a keepsake. $200

Coloring and Activity Books:

• We can take your art and/or photos and transform them into five
coloring/activity sheets that you can use and print and share. $275
• Mid-level option: We can gather many of the sheets into a
24-page coloring/activity book. $800
• Top-level option: We can use your unique family information to
create puzzles, such as crossword puzzles and word searches.
$1,000

Kiss Goodbye:

We can interview you to write the letter, then create a
beautifully designed version: $200

Do you have a book idea?
We also can help you write and publish your book,
including children's books, young adult books,
novels, memoirs, and nonfiction books.
For more information, contact Jennifer Bright,
founding CEO of Bright Communications, at
jennifer@brightcommunications.net or 610-216-0913.

About Bright Communications

Bright Communications LLC is a woman- and veteran-owned independent publishing company in the Lehigh Valley, Pennsylvania. Jennifer Bright founded Bright Communications LLC in 2004, fueled by her love of books and helping people.

Over the years, the company has grown from a small one-woman business providing editorial services to other publishing companies to a robust organization employing more than 25 independent professionals and publishing more than 35 books a year in most book categories, including fiction, health, inspiration, parenting, memoir, and children's books.

Our efficient, effective process takes authors from idea all the way through to finished books. We create print, eBook, and audiobook editions, and our books are available everywhere books are sold.

Our passion is helping authors and visionary brands bring their books to life. We make publishing easy—and fun!

We offer many programs, including:

- Self-publishing assist program
- Four publishing packages
- Commemorative books
- Collaborative books
- Wandering Writers Workshops
- Memory and Legacy Preservation Program
- Bright Communications Franchising: The first book publishing franchise!

Let's talk about your book! Contact us for a free brainstorming session, to ask questions, and to learn how we can help you bring your book to life!

Jennifer Bright
Founding CEO, Bright Communications
jennifer@brightcommunications.net
610-216-0913